POSITIVE PEER GROUPS

SHARON SCOTT

Copyright © 1988 by
Human Resource Development Press, Inc.
22 Amherst Road, Amherst, Massachusetts 01002
(413) 253-3488 (Mass.)
1-800-822-2801 (outside Mass.)

First Edition, First printing, April, 1985
                Second printing, September, 1985

Library of Congress Cataloging in Publication Data

International Standard Book No. 0-87425-065-X

Dedicated to
TEACHERS, COUNSELORS, AND VOLUNTEERS
Everywhere
Who Have or Are Developing
POSITIVE PEER GROUPS

About the Author

Sharon Scott is an internationally recognized lecturer, licensed professional counselor, and a frequent national radio and talk show guest. She is president of Sharon Scott and Associates, a Dallas-based firm offering training and consulting services to school districts, counseling agencies, law enforcement agencies, religious groups, and parent and youth groups. She has developed many innovative programs during her eighteen-year counseling career, including implementing positive peer groups in numerous school districts nationwide. She was featured on the nationally televised "Hour Magazine" with Gary Collins discussing the success of these groups.

Sharon Scott is the author of two widely acclaimed books, *Peer Pressure Reversal: An Adult Guide to Developing a Responsible Child* and *How to Say No and Keep Your Friends*. These books have received endorsements from the U.S. Department of Education, Boy Scouts of America, Parents' Resource Institute for Drug Education (PRIDE), National Federation of Parents, Narcotics Education, Inc., and Texans' War on Drugs. She has trained more than one hundred thousand adults and youth in her proven peer pressure reversal techniques. Her next book, *When to Say Yes!*, will be published soon.

Sharon Scott writes a "Positive Parenting" column for school newsletters and has been featured in a video about managing negative peer pressure, *Like a Roaring Lion*. She is the recipient of numerous awards including the 1987 Professional Writing Award presented by the Texas Association for Counseling and Development, the 1987 Heart of America Award presented by Lafayette Community Commitment, and a 1982 certificate of appreciation presented by Texas governor Bill Clements. She holds a master's degree in human relations and community affairs and a bachelor's degree in sociology. In addition, she has more than four hundred hours of postgraduate training with Dr. Robert R. Carkhuff, author of more than fifty books on helping and human relations.

Prior work experience includes seven years with the Dallas Police Department as director of the First Offender Program, which became a national model for delinquency prevention and youth rehabilitation. It was here that she first realized the intensity of negative peer pressure and that peers were the single most important influence on a child's decision to break the law. In response, she has spent the better part of her career developing skills and programs to turn negative peer pressure into positive peer pressure.

Preface

Having spent the better part of my counseling career researching and developing skills to help youth resist negative peer pressure by teaching them *how* to say no, it is with excitement that I now turn to focus on programs to encourage positive peer pressure.

One of the most powerful influences in youth's lives is their peers. Fred Beauvais, a Colorado State University psychologist, in his study of three hundred fifty midwestern eleventh and twelfth graders, found that friends' habits have at least five times more impact on teen drug use than other lifestyle factors.

Youth like the idea of helping their friends, and with proper training and organization can have a powerful, positive impact on friends. The concept of peer helpers is not new, but I hope that this book gives you some inspiration, motivation, and specific program ideas to develop a positive peer group at your school, or give you some new ideas should you already have one in place.

We need to help today's youth move from the *me* generation to the *we* generation. Positive peer groups can show them the way!

There are several individuals who I wish to thank: all the sponsors and students in peer support groups that I have helped to develop, as I have learned so much from them; my secretary, Terry Colvin, for hours of transcribing; my mentors, Dr. Robert R. Carkhuff and Dr. Tom Collingwood; my publisher; and clients, friends, family, and husband John, who continue to support and encourage me.

December 1987   Sharon Scott
Dallas, Texas

TABLE OF CONTENTS

1.

YEA!

POSITIVE

PEER

GROUPS

What are *positive peer groups*? Positive peer groups are most commonly developed in schools with the idea of making students more aware of and sensitive to other students' needs and bringing about some positive changes in the attitudes of the student body. Schools must function in some ways like a supportive family that offers a caring atmosphere. There are other systems that can use positive peer groups, including child care group homes, detention facilities, mental health settings, but this book will focus on schools. There would be few variations, however, in a positive peer group in these other settings.

It is estimated that in any school there are twenty percent positive leaders, twenty percent negative leaders, with the remaining sixty percent as followers. Positive peer groups are designed to develop skills in *more* students to enable them to counteract negative peer pressure as well as to establish peer support groups with fellow students. One might even say that a long-term goal of positive peer groups is to develop a *mentor* or leadership program. Positive peer groups for youth are based on the principles of successful adult positive peer groups, such as Weight Watchers, Alcoholics Anonymous, and Gamblers Anonymous. Some youth may fear seeking traditional services of help—school counselors, teachers, doctors, parents—and the positive peer group gives them a viable alternative.

This book will focus on the development of such groups and will highlight six exemplary programs.

These groups of youth and their sponsors often show great creativity in their projects and are sincerely dedicated to helping other students in their school. One of my favorite projects was produced by the SWAT (Students Working All Together) team at Trinity High School in Hurst-Euless-Bedford I.S.D. They called the project DOA. Concerned about the drinking and driving that frequently occurs over spring break (in Texas, especially by youth who go to South Padre Island on the Gulf Coast), the SWAT team designed and put up posters in the halls depicting the lower half of people's bodies (all you could see were legs: father in trousers, mother in skirt, kids in tennis shoes, etc.) with a tag on each person's toe that read "DOA" (a term meaning "dead on arrival," used by hospitals upon admission of someone deceased). These posters, although morbid, stimulated a lot of curiosity. Announcements over the public address system introduced this family and invited students to attend a presentation the week before spring break to learn what happened to this family during spring break. The narrated slide show featured the family packing for a trip, leaving, being hit by a car driven by drinking teens, being admitted to the hospital, and so forth. Several family members were listed in critical condition, but all survived in the end. The narrator said, "DOA can mean two things: dead on arrival or drive on alive. It's up to you." The audience was urged to not drink and to come back from spring break. Those who signed a commitment to do that received a keychain with "DOA" on it. Most of the students participated.

Some people may wonder why there is a need for such positive peer groups. They have only to examine how significantly our society has changed over the past fifteen to thirty years to realize the necessity for these groups. If you are thirty-five or older, reflect back on your youth. It probably has some similarities to mine.

I grew up in Denison, Texas, with both parents and with grandparents, aunts, uncles, and cousins nearby. My mother was a full-time homemaker, so was always around. My father got home from work about 5:15 p.m., and we always had evening meals together. We had only one TV and we watched it together. Sundays consisted of church, drives around Lake Texoma, and *Walt Disney, Ed Sullivan*, and *Bonanza* in the evening. We knew our neighbors and often we would sit outside in the evenings with them. I had a cocker spaniel, Pudgie, and a parakeet, Pepper, and was taught to love animals and nature. Role models were parents and teachers, Doris Day and John Wayne. It was a slower, calmer time, when kids could be kids.

Do you remember:
- Catching lightning bugs in a jar (and later letting them go because you didn't want them to die)?
- Enjoying ice cream socials (and your seat getting cold as you sat on the freezer while someone *hand*-cranked it)?
- Lying on grassy lawns with the family and trying to locate the Big Dipper?
- Playing simple (no cost, at home) games such as hide-and-seek, croquet, badminton, hopscotch?
- Watching family TV programs such as *Leave It*

to Beaver, *I Love Lucy*, *Father Knows Best*, and *Ozzie and Harriet*, whereby our parents' values were reinforced?

I doubt if you have memories that include:

- First-grade group slumber parties;
- Designer clothes (our labels were inside our clothes!);
- Your own phone at age thirteen;
- A new car given to you because you lived to age sixteen (I got a charm bracelet!);
- Multiple televisions (that separate us and often glamorize unhealthy things), VCRs (where R- and X-rated material comes right into the home), and microwave ovens (that give us the luxury of "grazing" in shifts).

Kids are growing up very fast and are having to face difficult, even adult, decisions at a much earlier age. Most adults over the age of thirty-five did not have to make their first decisions about drinking with friends until their late teens, somewhere between seventeen and twenty-one. The average age for youth making that same decision nowdays is twelve and a half. Negative peer pressure is usually the motivator. Back in the fifties and sixties, when "the guys" would go out and drink, perhaps as many as six would share one six-pack. Nowdays, if you see a group of six guys out drinking, each would probably have his own six-pack. We see not only that drinking is occurring at an earlier age, but also in larger proportions.

Drinking, however, remains but one of many problems that youth are facing today, as these alarming statistics show:

- One out of four students drops out of high school.
- A teenager commits suicide every ninety minutes.
- Four out of ten teenagers become pregnant.
- Of the roughly nine million persons who have become problem drinkers in this country, 3.3 million are teenagers.
- Forty-nine percent of high school students drink in cars.
- One hundred thousand elementary school students get drunk at least once each week.
- Drug use by sixth graders has tripled over the last decade.
- Cocaine deaths have tripled in just five years.

In 1985 the National Institute on Drug Abuse found that sixty-one percent of twenty-five thousand high school seniors surveyed reported using drugs at least once. A recent study reported in the 1986 U.S. Department of Education booklet, "What Works: Schools Without Drugs," says that teenagers contacting a cocaine hotline revealed that fifty-seven percent had bought most of their drugs at school.

Another study printed in the Winter 1987 PRIDE Newsletter, conducted by the Fullerton (California) Police Department and the California Department of Education, shows the drastic change in problems with student behavior. In the 1940s the top five problems were:

1. Talking
2. Chewing gum
3. Making noise
4. Running in the halls

5. Getting out of turn in line.

In the 1980s the top five problems are:

1. Drug abuse
2. Alcohol abuse
3. Pregnancy
4. Suicide
5. Rape.

These statistics are not meant to depress us, overwhelm us, or make us feel hopeless. They are intended to give us an urgency to the commitment and dedication that is needed to solve these problems.

Historically, our schools' attitude toward these growing problems and how to resolve them has gone through levels of development. Our schools, like our communities, often initially denied that the problems existed, hoping that the problems were not "that bad" or were not their responsibility. As the problems increased, however, most schools were forced to search frantically for answers.

Providing drug information, for example, was tried, and later we learned that it alone did not reduce the use of drugs, but may even have led to an increase in use. Values clarification was introduced, yet the problems magnified.

A current phase in development is appropriately an awareness campaign that has adopted the theme "Just Say No." Rallies and walks against drugs have been held to reinforce responsible decision making of our youth and to encourage others to stand up for what is right and healthy. Just Say No clubs, composed mainly of children aged seven to fourteen, have been organized in schools. The clubs provide education on the "gateway" drugs—alcohol, tobacco, and marijuana. The children practice saying no in skits, songs, cheers, etc. In July 1986 the Just Say No Foundation was formed to provide a national link for all Just Say No clubs through the distribution of materials and information. The foundation describes its program as being neither a formal curriculum nor a highly structured approach. Emphasis is on having fun, but the message is clear: drinking, smoking, and using drugs are wrong; every drug is potentially harmful; there is no "responsible" use of illicit drugs and no "responsible" use of alcohol or tobacco by minors.

In 1985 I wrote the book *Peer Pressure Reversal: An Adult Guide to Developing a Responsible Child* to share information on *how* we can teach youth to say no yet still be liked. I began developing the peer pressure reversal technique in 1974 in response to seeing so many youth who "know better" getting arrested. At that time I was with the Dallas Police Department's First Offender Program, and I began seeing that the number-one reason why kids were making bad decisions, including breaking laws, was because they did not know what to say to their friends when begged, bribed, dared, or challenged. This tendency has been reinforced by the more than fifty thousand youth that I have personally trained in my peer pressure reversal techniques. They explain that it continues to be hard to just say no to those that pressure them because it is the very people whom they want to like them that influence them the most: best friends, popular kids, older youth, and boyfriend or girlfriend.

Results of the First Offender Program between 1974 and 1987 bear out the effectiveness—reducing recidivism (repeat offenders)—of teaching youth the decision-making techniques of peer pressure reversal. Of the 8,533 delinquent youth who completed the program, there was an eighty percent success rate (not rearrested). Whereas for the 1,067 who dropped out of the program, the success rate was only thirty-eight percent.

And in a prevention program for nondelinquent youth at Webb Middle School in Garland, Texas, we reduced behavior problems in the school following peer pressure reversal training. My associates and I trained ninety-nine percent of the 1,070-member student body, faculty, and a majority of the parents, and there were significant decreases in most categories of referrals to the principal's office. Figure 1 reflects the percentage of change comparing the month before and the month following the peer pressure reversal training, and the percentage of change compared to the same months the previous year (base rate = 1986).

The results of referrals for drugs stayed the same as the previous year—only one referral for the months compared. However, we did have one student within one hour of completing the training go to the counselor's office seeking help for her drug use. She also turned in drugs she had in her locker. This was done solely through her own thinking following the workshop!

Peer pressure reversal training is highly successful in helping youth resist negative peer pressure. In this book we will go beyond that train-

Figure 1. Results of peer pressure reversal training at Webb Middle School.

Offense	% Decrease	% Decrease From Base Rate
Misbehavior on Bus	25.0	133.3
Threat to Students	75.0	25.0
Not Following Directions	37.5	55.1
Skipped Detention	4.0	25.3
Disruptive Activity	17.7	79.9

ing into a higher level of functioning: where we will teach youth when to say yes and how to help one another. We will show them how to get from the *me* generation to the *we* generation. If our world is ever to surmount its problems and if we are to have peace, then people, states, and nations must become interdependent.

A hierarchy of levels in managing negative peer pressure would resemble Figure 2.

As you prepare to develop peer group programs in your school or school district, you may want to plan the operation long-term, that is, over several years, moving from awareness to skill acquisition to a mentor-type program.

You may be wondering whether your school needs a positive peer group. If your school is experiencing problems with truancy, drugs, and alcohol, as so many schools are, it could benefit by such a group. Lawrence Harville, director of Hurst-

Figure 2. Managing negative peer pressure.

↑	5	Helping networks (communitywide effort)
Winners	4	Getting away positive (positive peer groups)
Survivors	3	Getting away clean (peer pressure reversal)
Losers	2	Getting away negative (say no, leave only alternatives)
↓	1	Getting caught (controlled by others)

Euless-Bedford I.S.D.'s Alternative Education Program, which is the last disciplinary resort before expulsion, attributes the decrease in violations of the school's drug abuse policy to the highly visible antidrug campaign presented by students as well as administrators. (You will hear more about its SWAT team later.) One, however, should not wait for problems to begin or become serious to form a positive peer group. Positive peer groups are ideally used as a prevention, rather than an intervention, technique. The schools where I have developed such groups have been in various degrees of need.

There are numerous short-term goals of positive peer groups. These include teaching the students the skills of handling negative peer pressure, so that they can serve as role models for other students. By acting as role models, possibly even as trainers, positive peer group members can help other students deal with negative peer pressure.

Another goal is to help new students become assimilated quickly into the school and become comfortable; also, identification and support of lonely or isolated students. A significant goal of positive peer groups is to make the public aware of the dangers that most adolescents are going to face during their preteen and teenage years, especially concerning harmful effects of illegal drugs and alcohol.

Such short-term goals, when met by the implementation of positive peer groups in schools, yield long-term benefits as well. Effective positive peer groups can reduce serious problems in schools, including drugs, alcohol, vandalism, absenteeism, fighting, and gossip and cliques, and make the schools a more pleasant place for all. Younger students entering these schools, then, will not hear as many horror stories and have less fear in their middle school and high school years.

Many youth recently graduated from elementary school have a fearful summer before they begin middle school. They fantasize being forced to drink alcohol or use other drugs, being beaten up or knifed, being locked in lockers, as well as not being able to find their classrooms in a larger school and having to move from class to class. Positive peer group members can allay these fears.

Positive peer groups can be implemented at different grade levels: upper elementary, middle school, or high school. Ideally, it would be wise to put such groups into all of these different grade levels, but if one can not, the choice may be between which school has the greatest need and which school would afford the highest degree of initial success. It may be easier and more effective to begin a group in a simpler, less troublesome setting than to begin it where there are extremely serious problems. The principle of making your program successful is to start with the smaller problems first and build to more serious problems as you become more experienced in developing and implementing such programs.

Some school districts where I have developed such programs have begun the program at just one school; others at certain grade levels at all schools; and still others on a districtwide basis. Many have relied only on faculty and staff involvement; others have taken a communitywide approach and have involved community agencies and organizations as sponsors and supporters. Both approaches can be effective and both meet different needs. We will look at such ideas later in this book as we examine specific programs.

2.

ADULT

SPONSORS:

KEY TO

SUCCESS

It is imperative that the adults selected to serve as sponsors for student peer groups be excited about the concept, dedicated, and energetic. Organizational skills are obviously extremely helpful as is experience in communicating and organizing large groups of youth. At times I have known the adult sponsors to meet all the listed criteria except for experience in working with large groups of youth. I have seen some of those same people become frustrated by their inability to get the attention of a large group of youth. Adult leadership is critical to the success of peer group programs, as it can help keep the groups organized and *alive*. We will discuss in this chapter the selection and the training of the adult sponsors.

If your positive peer group is developed as part of the school program, you will naturally want to use teachers, counselors, or administrators who support this plan. I do not recommend that the principal or some other person assign this responsibility to someone who he or she assumes might be interested in such a program. Even by asking for volunteers, one does not always get the people who are really most interested; some may volunteer only to get Brownie points. I recommend that some kind of presentation to the faculty and staff be made about the possibility of developing a positive peer group in the school. You can ask for volunteers to talk with you at a later date if they are interested. Their duties in the program should be carefully explained to them as well as the time involved. You may also have some people in mind who you think would be especially good for this program. You might want to talk with them on an

individual basis and let them know, in a compli-
mentary way, of your high opinion of their qualifi-
cations. There are some people who like to volunteer and there are others who like to feel that
they were handpicked because of their skills.

After the adult sponsors have been selected and
before starting the program, some training and
program development ideas need to be outlined.
Each adult sponsor should familiarize himself or
herself with positive peer groups by reading this
book. It would also be beneficial for each adult
sponsor to read my book, *Peer Pressure Reversal:
An Adult Guide to Developing a Responsible Child*
(Human Resource Development Press, 1985). This
book will help familiarize adult sponsors with the
intensity and kinds of negative peer pressure that
the average adolescent encounters. It will also
give them a lot of ideas on training of the student
peer groups, some of which will be overviewed in
this book, but not to the degree that is outlined in
that book.

The adult sponsors will have to decide on the
selection process of the students, the training of
students, the frequency of meetings once the
students are trained, the location and times of
such meetings, and other factors. The sponsors
will also have to decide on how they are going to
measure the success of the program. Some
schools do their evaluation in a loose manner
whereby they judge attitude change and the atmosphere in the school before and after the forma-
tion of positive peer groups. Most schools *sense*
improvement, believing that the peer groups are
having a favorable impact. Other schools, how-

ever, want more definitive test criteria to substantiate the impact of peer groups on specific behavioral problems. If the positive peer group, for example, intended to affect truancy, that could easily be measured for several months before and after the group had begun to attack the problem. One would not want to measure the drinking problem in the school, though, unless that was actually a goal that the positive peer group was actively trying to affect. In other words, you would measure only those behaviors that the group are actively seeking to influence.

The sponsors need to come to an agreement on the method of selection of the students. The method can vary, from a simple system, such as the principal and counselor approving those asked to participate, to a more complex, thorough process, such as a survey conducted of the entire student body or a certain percentage of it. The survey form could include questions such as "What student would you talk to if you had a problem?" "What students in this school do you trust the most?" These types of questions are intended to deter the students from putting down names of just the most popular students, and to answer with names of students with whom they really feel comfortable talking. Another method of selection is to have a committee, composed of the principal, counselor, teachers, and parents, name students who they feel would contribute to the positive peer group. Another technique is to conduct interviews with students. This type of selection might take more time but would help the adults ascertain which students really have interest in and time for the program. In chapter 3 we will explore the types of students that adults need to select in order to build a strong positive peer group.

Another area that the adults will need to address is the cost involved in developing a positive peer group. Some schools function on no budget at all, knowing, for example, that the small amount of material that they may need for reproduction can be done on school paper. Some schools may decide to develop the program solely using their own personnel at no additional cost to them. Others might want to bring in an outside consultant to kick off the program. The initial excitement stirred by an experienced training consultant is a persuasive show of commitment to the program on the part of the school and promotes more serious participation of both adults and youth. Schools should consider alternative fundraising ideas:

- Obtain donations from the PTA, Junior League, Rotary, and other civic organizations.
- Mail proposed ideas to local businesses and request donations.
- Ask parents to solicit donations from organizations to which they belong or make donations themselves.
- Sponsor bake sales, dances for youth, dinners for adults.
- Collect bottles and aluminum cans and turn them in for cash.
- Solicit funds from organized community groups that promote chemical-free lives.

School districts can get other community agencies or organizations involved as well, and may decide not only to ask for their support but also for their commitment in ''adopting'' a school. Such organizations may assign a volunteer to be present at each of the group's meetings. Organizations that might participate include service clubs such as the Junior League, Lions, and Kiwanis, the city council and local police department, YMCA or YWCA, PTA, the ministerial alliance, and parent peer groups or other groups devoted to drug-free lifestyles.

3.

YOUTH: ENTHUSIASM ENTERS

In this chapter we will discuss the selection and training of the youth for the positive peer groups. As previously mentioned, the method of selecting students can vary. What is important is that a cross-section of the student body be represented. That is, you need to select leaders of the *various* peer groups. In this way all neighborhoods, academic standards, interests and abilities, and degrees of social interaction are represented. To select only leaders that may be the best students or the most popular youth would be a mistake, as these youth, in general, can lead only their peer groups and others would not benefit by the positive peer groups.

There is one important criterion to positive peer group qualification: each student should have "a heart of gold." I know of no other way to describe this, except that the youth need to be sincerely interested in helping their friends and benefiting the school through their commitment to these groups. It is okay for youth participating in the group to have some "rough edges," as long as they could be positive representatives if given support and encouragement. I am not recommending, however, that a student who is an active drug user be selected for this program, as generally the student's attitude is so poor, and even often anti-establishment, that he or she would not be a good representative for this group. Youth who are recovering users with many months of drug-free living can be excellent candidates, as they can offer insight to others about self-judgment and proper decision making. I have often seen kids who used to drink alcohol on the weekends make a commitment to stop drinking and serve then as excellent representatives for their peer groups. If you are implementing one of these programs at the high school level, it might be very difficult to select students who do not drink at all because drinking is so prevalent at the secondary school level. These youth need to know, however, that they must eliminate use of chemicals and make better decisions, so that they can be good role models for their friends. Hypocritical behavior ("do as I say, not as I do") can destroy a group's credibility.

As you are selecting students, keep in mind that you need a group size of at least five percent of the student body. The smallest peer group that I have ever trained in a school is thirty students, with the largest *initially* trained being one hundred fifty.

Once a list of students has been made, now begins the process of talking to each of these students individually to ascertain his or her interest in the peer group. Stress that peer group participation requires dedication and takes priority over the student's other personal activities. During the discussion closely watch the student's reaction to your definition of peer group participation. If the student immediately starts telling you about his or her lengthy lists of other personal commitments, or wants to know exactly how long he or she will have to participate in this peer group or how much time it will take each week, these may be warning signs that this youth does not have the time or interest. As you are talking to the candidates, they should feel pride in being selected to participate and appear excited about such a program.

Some schools have required the participants to sign a form that they will not use alcohol or other illegal drugs, since being a part of this peer group puts them in a position of role models. This is optional, but obviously has some advantages by adding more obligation on the part of the student to make wise choices. Even if such a statement is not used, some schools may choose to make it mandatory that the student's parents are contacted to ascertain their willingness to allow their son or daughter to participate or are asked to sign a form agreeing to their child's participation in the peer group. (See appendix 1 for sample form.)

This next step is optional, but a nice gesture on the part of the adult sponsors. Some schools have an initial group meeting to welcome the students, introduce them to their fellow participants, as well as introduce them to the adult sponsors. This meeting could last anywhere from ten to thirty minutes. During this meeting it would be beneficial to state again the overall goal of the positive peer group, the responsibilities required of each member, and the commitment needed to make this program effective. An added point of encouragement could be a statement that this group is the first of its kind at the school and, if successful, could lead to an expanded positive peer group program in their school. In some school districts where student peer groups have been put in place, from upper elementary through high school, an added bonus to participation is the prospect of moving on to other positive peer groups at other schools within the district, thereby allowing the students to make new friends and continue being helpers to others.

The next step is to provide training to the student peer group. The areas recommended for training are two two-hour sessions: "How to Say No and Keep Your Friends: Decision Making for Ourselves" and "When to Say Yes: Decision Making to Help Others." These training sessions ideally should be covered on separate days and, if possible, several days apart, so that you do not overwhelm the students with too much information at one time.

The first part of the training, "How to Say No and Keep Your Friends: Decision Making for Ourselves," involves teaching the students my peer pressure reversal techniques. Even though these students are supposed to be leaders in their peer group, they are constantly being bombarded by negative peer pressure (and sometimes they are the ones *to* pressure). Every day they most likely face difficult decisions about copying homework, gossiping, perhaps skipping school, lying to their parents about where they are really going, and maybe even more serious situations including drugs, alcohol, and sexuality. So we must begin their training by giving them ways of saying no and saving face.

If the adult sponsor reads chapters one through three in *Peer Pressure Reversal: An Adult Guide to Developing a Responsible Child*, he or she will learn the basics of the technique as well as the training delivery involved to teach the students. I have also written a companion book for youth,

How to Say No and Keep Your Friends (Human Resource Development Press, 1986). Each student should read this book to understand the basics of managing negative peer pressure. Emphasize to the participants that in order to help others we must be able to help ourselves first. The success of the group is dependent on honesty of the members—hypocritical conduct can be harmful. Group members, for example, can not work on a campaign to discourage drinking and then drink on the weekend. Dedication, although difficult, must be stressed and is usually well received by the participants. (See appendix 2 for positive peer group application.)

Once both the adults and the youth have read the books, this first two-hour training session should be a time for the adults to share information about negative peer pressure and the use of peer pressure reversal. The first hour of the training should be confined to instruction and discussion. Teach and review what peer pressure is and why it is hard to say no to friends. Share with them a peer pressure situation that was difficult for you. Invite them to share some of their experiences; of course, remind them not to mention friends' names. Discuss from *How to Say No and Keep Your Friends* the ways described to manage negative peer pressure. Keep it upbeat, fast-paced, and fun. Remind them that in order to help others, we must be able to help ourselves.

After a short break, the second hour of the workshop should be filled with skits and role-play practices to give the youth an opportunity to use these skills. As the practice goes on it will be clearly seen that it is often difficult to get out of peer pressure traps. Some of the mistakes that you will likely see are students (1) taking too long to get out of trouble (it should take thirty seconds or less); (2) coming back to the peer rather than walking away from trouble after the peer pressures them with a line such as "Chicken" or "I thought you were my friend"; (3) attempting to debate their friend; and (4) being highly critical of the peer and starting a fight or argument. All of these instances will make it more difficult for the person to handle negative peer pressure. It is fun and beneficial for the observers to evaluate the decision makers by giving a signal of thumbs up, thumbs sideways, or thumbs down, depending on how they handled the situation. This practice keeps everyone involved and adds positive peer pressure to force the decision makers to handle the troubling situation well.

Peer pressure reversal involves preparing these students for a three-step decision-making process by which they can handle trouble effectively at a moment's notice. First, they will learn to become more aware of situations in which negative peer pressure is likely to occur and be able to identify trouble readily. Second, they will learn how and when to make quick, logical decisions rather than emotional judgments influenced by their friends' negative encouragement. Finally, and most important, they will learn ten different ways or styles of saying no to avoid trouble. It is important that each of the students identify at least three of the styles with which he or she is most comfortable.

We all have unique personalities and have our

own ways of avoiding trouble. Some people think that it may be enough to just say no or walk away from trouble; however, as previously mentioned, youth will tell you that it is most difficult to just say no or walk away from best friends, the popular gang, older kids, or boyfriend or girlfriend. These are the people with whom they are generally around the most. Therefore, we must teach them other ways to be able to get out of trouble and still feel like they have their friends and their dignity.

After an emphasis on being good role models, the second part of the training gets to the heart of what positive peer groups are all about: helping others. This training should be separated from the first part by at least a week, if possible. The text that the youth should have read and be familiar with is my book *When to Say Yes!* (Human Resource Development Press, 1988). This training should be conducted prior to any discussion of what the specific goals of this group are going to be or how to implement such goals. This training therefore can be titled "When to Say Yes—Decision Making to Help Others!" There are three major steps that youth should be taught at this point, through discussion and roleplay: checking out the scene, making a good decision, and acting to help others.

Check Out the Scene

In this particular step you are not just teaching students to check out the scene for troublesome situations that they should avoid, but to notice what is going on around them, such as if there are lonely or isolated students in their school. In the average school there are generally many students who eat by themselves in the cafeteria every day and who may go for days, even weeks, on end without anyone saying hello to them. New students may not be noticed and it is easy for them to get lost in the crowd. Ask the participants if they have ever been a new student. Many of them can identify with the fright and confused feelings they had the first days and weeks at their new school.

The other point to make is that they need to get beyond paying attention only to their own close peer group and be watchful of other things that are going on in the school. They should be alert to negative peer pressure among others, such as gossip or discussion of fighting or cheating. In essence, you are trying to get them to be more aware through observing and through listening about what is going on in their school, so that later they can make decisions about whether they can help and what form this help should take.

Consider sharing some real-life, even fictitious, situations as examples of good decision making. A story that I often tell is a true account that took place in a middle school. One of the girls in a positive peer group in that school noticed that every day as she left the cafeteria two girls, at opposite ends of the concourse, eating alone. One day the girl in the positive peer group decided to take a chance, and walked over to one of the girls and introduced herself, and made the comment about the two of them always sitting out there, eating lunch alone, and that they should really get to know each other. She told me that the girl giggled and said yes, it would be okay to meet the other girl. So the girl in the positive peer group walked over to the other side and introduced herself, said the same thing, and then brought the girls together. The end of the story is that each day as this girl would leave the cafeteria she saw these two girls eating lunch together. She had helped two lonely people make friends. A small thing in some ways, but very significant in others.

Make a Good Decision

In this step you are trying to get the students to think of the implications of what would happen if they did not make an attempt to help in negative peer pressure situations or if someone was being harmed or left out. You are not trying to teach the students to police the school, but to make them feel responsibility and judge for themselves when it is appropriate to intervene or make a positive comment to help another person. Sometimes all a person needs to make a good decision is somebody to encourage him or her in the right direction or to pull him or her away gently from a troublesome situation. Ask the participants to consider what would happen if they did not help, they will generally answer with "Nobody will help," which is sadly often the case.

Another story that I often share with peer group participants is one that happened as my husband John was driving home from work late one evening. It was a rainy night, and as he drove he noticed that a car ahead of him had stopped and the driver was out in front of his car looking down at the ground. He had hit a dog. The man told John that he didn't know what to do, since it was late and no vets were open. My husband offered to help. He suggested taking the dog nearby to our veterinary friend. The vet took a look at the dog and told them to take it to the clinic, only five minutes away, where he would operate. There the dog was cleaned, her wounds stitched, and she was given intravenous solutions. The vet said that he would not know until the next morning if the dog was going to make it. They left, and upon returning the next morning knew that the dog would survive. The problem now was to locate the dog's owner. So I got involved. I made and put up posters in the neighborhood, put an ad in the newspaper, and asked other veterinarians to identify the dog and its owner. That afternoon the owner called.

The point of this story is that many people were involved in helping in this situation. If the man who hit the dog had gone on his way, as some would have done, the dog would have surely died. If my husband had not stopped and helped the man locate a nearby vet, or if the vet had not agreed to go to work that night, the dog would not have lived. If I had not advertised for the owner to call about the dog, the dog would have had no home.

Act to Help Others

This step involves a presentation and discussion of both *individual* actions that each member of the positive peer group can take to help others in their school, as well as *group* activities that can be conducted to meet the same goal. Let's expand on these individual actions and group activities in chapter 4.

4.
POSITIVE
PEER
GROUP
GOALS

It is important that the participants feel the power that they can impact others even as individuals. We can encourage them that single thoughts and actions count. In order to encourage their joint efforts, it is also important that they realize the extra influence that group persuasion can have.

First we will look at *individual* actions that the members of peer groups can exhibit to improve the general attitude of the student body in their school. There are far too many suggested actions to enumerate here, but a few deserve special mention. It would be beneficial at this point to ask members of the group to generate their own ideas and for the adult sponsor to supplement these with his or her own. They should include greeting more people and being friendlier to more than just one's immediate peer group, eliminating gossip, occasionally inviting an isolated student to lunch, sincerely trying to listen to other people's problems, as well as going out of one's way to help new students.

An in-depth discussion of the skill of listening would be appropriate at this time. To begin the discussion, point out how we sometimes half listen to other people's problems and how we often talk about our own problems instead of listening to theirs. We often even try to top other people's problems with our own by saying, for example, "You think that's bad? Let me tell you what happened to me." We often fail to be physically attentive when another person is needing to be listened to: we may be looking around, leaning back in a too-relaxed posture, or even interrupting the discussion. Stress how important the skill of listening is, especially when someone is going through a crisis in his or her life, such as parents' divorce, loss of a boyfriend or girlfriend, or fear of failing a subject. And the group needs to know that one does not have to have the answer or solution to the problem (in fact, the person will have to solve his or her own problem), but active listening can be extremely beneficial in allowing the other person to think through his or her problem.

Also, there should be a discussion about increasing the amount of sincere compliments or praise statements given to others. We frequently give compliments only to our closest peer group, failing to realize that we all need to be praised, and many times we notice positive things others do but fail to mention them. We also can be guilty of the phony type of praise whereby all we do is focus in on someone's appearance and not on exemplary behavior. We must recognize that people always need positive statements about their behavior. Students often tell me that they rarely have anyone commend them for winning an award, playing an instrument well, making good grades, or other such activities. In fact, they sometimes receive put-down comments such as "Oh, you're just a brain. It's easy for you" or "Teacher's pet." Sometimes we tend to recognize the athletes or the beautiful people only for their talents. Sometimes we do give praise but the manner of our delivery is negative. For example, it might sound something like this: "You really did a good job on that English report. It's a lot better than the last one." You unknowingly have just reminded the person of his or her previous poor grade and have actually not given a praise statement.

There will be times when each person in the positive peer group will encounter a fellow student being criticized or extended an invitation to trouble. In such a situation the person can try to distract this fellow student away from the trouble or criticism, perhaps just by asking a simple question, relevant or not. A comment such as "Forget it. Let's go to class" is often enough to do the trick.

The number of *group* activities that peer group members could decide upon is limited only by their imagination, enthusiasm, and commitment. Following are some activities that I have seen implemented with success.

One method involves peer group members teaching the skills learned from my peer pressure reversal techniques to their own classmates or to students of lower school grades. High school students, for example, could train middle school or elementary school students. Trained middle school students could speak to graduating elementary school students about the pending transition between grades in order to placate their fears and assure their smoother entry into the new school.

I recall a particular middle school where the peer group students wanted to teach the peer pressure reversal techniques to their classmates. The sponsor said that they would have to get permission from the principal and, if they were given permission, figure out the logistics. The principal liked the idea but warned them that it would be difficult to teach youth of their same age, as their classmates would not necessarily want to listen and might not even think they needed to learn these skills. The students responded that these would be the youth that needed the skills the most. A wise and determined group of youth! The principal told them to develop their program and to show it to him in its entirety. The students broke up into teams and created and practiced their program. Two weeks later they returned to the principal, showed him their routine, and he immediately gave them permission to go into some of the health and physical education classes to make their presentation. At the outset they would walk into rooms of yawning, bored students who would be looking out the windows and acting as if they did not want to listen to the group. Nevertheless, the group continued. When they got to the part in their presentation in which volunteers were needed to perform in some skits, the students became enthusiastic and vied to participate. The group had obviously won over their peers. As I continue to see groups use this method, I am always excited by the results.

Some schools may decide to sponsor a newcomers club, whereby members of the positive peer group are assigned in pairs to help new students. During the first few weeks of school they direct the newcomers to their correct classes, introduce them to others, make sure they have someone to sit with at lunch, and assist in other ways to help the new students assimilate quickly into the school. Schools that have a high number of new students should implement such a program to avert the serious consequences of students' loneliness (e.g., dropouts and suicides).

At one school the students complained about the number of cliques on campus, and I suggested that their group sponsor a Meet Someone New at Lunch Day as a solution. They followed up on this suggestion. On the specified day, as the students came into the cafeteria, no one was allowed to sit at his or her usual table. Instead the students had to sit at tables designated by the first letter of their last name. They could have just as easily been assigned numbers. The idea was to force people to meet others who they normally would not have had the opportunity to know.

Positive peer group members have been known to tutor fellow students who are having difficulty in a particular subject. Here again we see peers helping peers who are potential dropouts and in need of support with their studies.

Schools could sponsor a play about negative peer pressure. The production would involve a lot of different talents: writing and editing, costumes and set design, advertising and marketing, and perhaps even film if the school has a video camera available. Some schools have become so active with this enterprise that the students actually travel around their county or state putting on their productions. Peer group members could sell tickets to the performance as a money-making project, with the proceeds used to invite guest speakers to their school or put toward some other beneficial measures to meet some of the goals of their group.

The peer group could sponsor an essay and/or art contest about the "Toughest Decision I Ever Made," "How I Handle Peer Pressure," or "Why I've Decided to Live Chemical Free." The members of the group could ask the teachers to make announcements about the program in class or announce it themselves over the school's public address system. They could design and put up posters in the school explaining the rules of the contest. Various community stores might donate prizes for the winners of the contest, such as records, dinners, tickets to events, and gift certificates. Adult sponsors, PTA members, or leading citizens could serve as judges. The point of such a project would be to generate discussion about negative peer pressure and what can be done to overcome it.

Positive peer groups may want to conduct a substance abuse campaign focusing on tobacco, alcohol, or other drugs, and make posters describing its harmful effects. Of the thousands of drug-using youth whom I have counseled over the years, the number-one reason for that first-time indulgence was "because my friends were." We need positive peer pressure to turn this around. During Drug Awareness Week the group could sponsor a guest speaker to discuss harmful effects of alcohol and other drug abuse or techniques of saying no. If a guest speaker is selected, that person should be an expert on the subject matter as well as experienced in making presentations to large audiences, particularly youth.

For secondary school students in particular, another idea might be for the positive peer group to invite a guest speaker (entertainer, caterer, etc.) to campus to talk about planning chemical-free parties that are fun. So many secondary students tell me that there are few parties that they are invited to where alcohol is not served. And many of these parties even have parents present who condone the use of teens drinking alcohol. Some youth seriously ask what one can do at a party where there is no alcohol. Parties at this age can be dull if entertainment is not planned or unappetizing food and unappealing drinks are served. Parties can be especially fun if the hosts and even the guests have been taught entertainment ideas and easy food suggestions, particularly how to make good-tasting, nonalcoholic beverages (*mock*tails, not cocktails!).

Positive peer groups may want to align their goals with those of national programs, such as Project Graduation. Project Graduation began in 1980 in one small Maine community that had been struck by eleven alcohol-related deaths in one weekend. The idea is for high school students to plan a safe all-night graduation activity that all graduating seniors would want to attend.

Unbelievable as it may seem, some parents will resist the idea. So be prepared. A Canadian group once told me that a number of parents resented their plans, as the parents said that it was a night of celebration for their kids and they wanted them to "live it up." We all want that, but we all want them to live beyond that night also. I suggested to the youth that they continue with their planned celebration and consider getting students, faculty, and parents to sign a petition in support of it. It is obvious that we need to educate parents who may unwittingly condone illegal or harmful activities.

Some peer group members and other students have suggested that their parents get more involved in school activities. The school could sponsor a family night. The positive peer group could help start a parent peer group. The parents could sponsor picnics and parties. We should all follow what I call the fifty-one percent principle: if we can get fifty-one percent of the students not to drink, fifty-one percent of the students to go to supervised parties, fifty-one percent of the students to support school activities, then we have the majority as a positive influence and it makes it easier for others to join in on such healthy activities.

One way to reinforce positive peer group identity—at the very least, to ensure the members' continuing commitment to and sense of pride in the program—is for the school to issue business cards. The business cards would carry the name of the group, logo (if any), and perhaps an inviting message, such as "Call me. I care" or "Call me if I can help." Space should be left for the member to write his or her name and phone number. These cards could be presented to any fellow student in suspected need.

Individual pride and group identity are in the limelight at school-sponsored rallies as well, at which both youth and adults express their support for drug-free living. They may want to wear colorful arm bands or tie ribbons around trees and have store owners put ribbon bows on their front doors.

Aware of the media impact on impressionable

youth, perhaps in a general assembly the peer group will want to discuss the effects of media on our lifestyles and talk about truth in advertising. They could act out in skits what commercials should *really* be saying. These role plays can be hilarious, but make a point. Or the group can use their own media, the school newspaper, to sponsor a Dear Abby type of column answering questions about teen life.

Some schools may want their positive peer groups to join national youth groups. Some of these organizations publish excellent newsletters that your group could subscribe to and share the information. Fundraising proceeds could be used to send representatives to these organizations' national conferences. (See appendix 7 for a list of resources.)

Now that the students have received their training, and the adults have received their training, they are ready to decide on program implementation.

5.

PLAN

OF

ACTION

As the group now begins to meet formally, the first session or two should involve a lengthy discussion of problem areas as the students perceive them. For a positive peer group to be successful, solutions to problems and the setting of goals need to be generated by the members themselves. The adults will surely want to add any ideas that have not been mentioned, but be aware that the adult sponsors do not set the specific program that the group will attempt to implement. The program in that case would be an adult program and the students' desire and enthusiasm to implement it would be drastically reduced. Depending on the number of youth participating, it may be helpful to start with small groups and later combine into large groups.

The session begins with students listing problems as someone writes them on a blackboard or notepad for all to see. Avoid discussing which problems are more serious than others. All that is being attempted at this point is to expand and list as many problem areas as they see. The list could include such problems as alcohol and other drug use, truancy, fighting, cheating, gossip and cliques, teenage pregnancy, drag racing, dress code, and even lack of school spirit.

Once the list has been expanded, now is the time to decide on some priorities. (See appendix 3.) If the group came up with, say, five problem areas, it is unlikely that the group could attack all of them in the coming school year. The students should decide on one or two problem areas that they want to address: either the most serious problems on their list or the less serious problems that offer a higher probability of success. Though drinking off campus, for example, might be considered an extremely serious problem, the students had better select an on-campus issue over which they would have more control. The adult sponsor needs to differentiate the possibilities for them.

If the positive peer group is a large one, it can be divided into teams, with each team working on a particular problem area. Once the goals have been decided upon, they should be put in writing and posted, perhaps on large poster board, at the front of the room during each meeting in order to remind the students to keep to their goals. The group, or representatives of the group, along with adult sponsors, should meet with the principal to explain the specific goals and obtain his or her support at this stage.

Now comes the task of developing methods to implement these goals. (Refer to chapter 4 for examples of group activities.) A creative group, duly encouraged, will come up with many ideas.

Now that the students know their specific goals and have devised ways of accomplishing these goals, they will surely want to develop a creative name for their group. I have worked with groups who called themselves SWAT (Students Working All Together), STOP (Students Thinking of Peers), SWAPP (Students Working Against Peer Pressure), NURDS (Never Underestimate Really Determined Students), TRY (Teen Relations and You), TAD (Teens Against Drugs), H_2O (Help to Others), STAR (Students Trained in Awareness and Resistance), and FUN (Friends U Need).

Next there should be a discussion of frequency of meetings and at what time of day these meetings should be held. It is suggested that meetings be held at least every two weeks and times of day could be what is most convenient for the entire group—during lunch, before school, after school, or evening. Note, however, that meetings held close to school hours are better attended.

I strongly advise against turning positive peer groups into social clubs. Members of the group are not an elite, handpicked, popular crowd; they are committed individuals who are working toward positive peer pressure and helping others. They are also hopeful that as years go by the size of the group will increase, so that instead of composing five percent of the student body, the group may constitute ten or even fifteen percent. It is also unwise to let the group select officers, for then it would be too much like a social club. To maintain control of the meeting, the group may divide itself into teams, which would take turns in leading the discussion on progress reports.

Not only the adult sponsors but also the students should be involved in evaluating the progress of the peer group. Should there be a problem with attendance, some criteria may have to be established to ensure participation, perhaps a rule that a certain percentage of meetings must be attended without exception (except illness). What is required, ideally, is everyone's commitment to the group, which functions as an organized committee.

As months go by, further ideas can be added and other goals can be worked on, if time allows. From meeting to meeting the students must make specific suggestions on how to accomplish the goal, otherwise the approach will be too loose. If there are other schools in your district that also have positive peer groups, you may want to plan an annual sharing of ideas with the other students' peer groups. And don't forget to get media publicity. (See appendix 4.)

6.

SIX

MODEL

GROUPS

This chapter will present an overview of selected effective positive peer groups (all in Texas) that Sharon Scott and Associates has helped to develop, train, and implement. We will focus on techniques and unusual or creative program ideas.

SWAT (Students Working All Together)

The SWAT program began in September 1986, with the training of sixty students from Trinity and L.D. Bell high schools plus sponsor training of two coordinators and fifty advisors. Both schools, located between Dallas and Fort Worth in the Hurst-Euless-Bedford Independent School District, targeted alcohol and other abuse as primary problems to address. Response to the program was so great that several months later I trained an additional sixty students and more advisors. The group of initial advisors were teachers and counselors, but later included interested parents in the second training group.

In May 1987 Trinity High School's positive peer group was awarded first prize (a personal computer system with color monitor and printer, at the Project Graduation contest sponsored by a variety of Dallas County and Tarrant County organizations. The 122 schools that entered the contest were judged on their year-long efforts to promote awareness of the dangers of chemical substance abuse based on the creativity of their programs, the number of students reached, the educational value, and the presentations they gave to the executive committee behind Project Graduation. Additionally, Trinity students took eleven of the top thirteen places (including second and third place) awarded to individuals.

Counselor Jan Laramore, coordinator of the SWAT team at Trinity High School, attributes training, teamwork among advisors, interesting activities and projects, plus positive reinforcement as the factors that most motivated her group. From thirty students, the group has grown to one hundred forty-five in eight months, with one hundred fifty more on the "contact" list.

Laramore believes that for youth and adults to do well in such a program they must care about others, be sensitive to the needs of others and not be afraid to reach out, act as positive role models on campus, work hard, and be firmly committed to helping youth overcome negative peer pressure.

The SWAT team encountered little resistance. There was some teasing initially by other students of those in SWAT. That had been discussed in our original training sessions and the SWAT members used their skills: ignore and/or react in a positive manner. Laramore says that there continues to be a hub of true workers. For those who have done the most work, positive recognition before the entire student body was given. The only other problem encountered was "lack of time to do all that we would like to do," she adds, and "this has not been solved."

One of their most rewarding programs involved a presentation and follow-up visit by a three-member SWAT team focusing on drug abuse, positive peer pressure, and an overview of my peer pressure reversal techniques. These presentations were conducted for all 1,250 sixth-grade students in the district during March and April 1987. The SWAT teams were pleasantly surprised by the way the sixth graders looked up to them and listened. In fact, one appreciative sixth-grade class later trained a third-grade class!

The SWAT team has also been involved with pep rally skits and assemblies about saying no to chemicals. Guest speakers have included famous sports heroes based locally who spoke on the dangers of alcohol and other drugs. Another of their special activities was the Reach-Out contest. To get a ticket to the Christmas party, each SWAT member had to invite at least one nonmember who could resist peer pressure. The person bringing the most nonmembers received a prize. The team also sponsored a Project Graduation Week and held different activities each day (SWAT Fair, radio station disc jockey visit, film, fun-run, etc.). An After-Graduation Chemical-Free Party for the seniors is planned; purchase of tickets "costs" only a signed commitment to be chemical-free before and during this party. In addition, to promote their activities and gather community support, members often show to clubs and organizations a videotape that they made.

Kay Baker, assistant principal of L.D. Bell High School, says that SWAT at her school is definitely growing, with tremendous interest among the students and adults as well. There are four main sponsors with a total of seventy-five adults working with the group and one hundred twenty youth trained. This was a timely program, as students, faculty, and parents saw a great need for it. The school and the community, says Baker, made a commitment in striving to enable the students to better cope with the complexities and the pressures of today's society.

She adds, "We not only felt but were shown, through observation of Sharon Scott's program, that life skills were taught. . .to better enable young people to say no with confidence and ease. The fact that no is and can be acceptable was stressed throughout her training. . . . In addition, the program enhanced individual self-esteem, a vital aspect in developing capable and productive young people."

Her group has been most excited by the positive peer pressure programs presented to the sixth-grade students, and has been particularly successful in role playing as a means of sharing information with other groups. With the assistance of adult sponsors, the members wrote a script in which role playing is a major component.

Baker believes that for youth to do well in peer groups they must be committed to the program, have high self-esteem in order to share the skills in peer pressure reversal, and be able to speak with ease before a group or an individual in order to impart this type of information successfully.

STOP (Students Thinking of Peers)

I was called in during the 1983–84 school year to help the Plano Independent School District develop and implement a positive peer group program. Due to a tremendous growth spurt in this community (now 114,000 population), many new students were moving in and having trouble assimilating in their schools. The town had also tragically experienced a large number of teenage suicides and wanted to develop a support system of students for students.

Initially, I trained from thirty to sixty youth in each of the six middle schools (grades six through eight) in the district. Because of the program's success at this level, I was asked to extend training to all high schools (grades nine and ten) and senior high schools (grades eleven and twelve). The following fall it was offered to upper elementary students (grades four and five). I have continued as a consultant to this district for its highly successful program.

Mike Cavender, formerly director of student services for Plano I.S.D. and now president of the Dallas Challenge, Inc., states that Plano Junior League support and funding, quality training, PTA support, and administrative support were the factors that most motivated their program. The problem areas that STOP hoped to impact were suicide, chemical use, and negative peer pressure. Some of the activities designed to achieve those goals include new-student orientation (buddy system) and parties for newcomers, students teaching classes on my peer pressure reversal techniques, role playing, posting positive slogans in halls, and theater productions. At some schools STOP members invite new or lonely students to meetings. Some of the schools have encouraged students and parents to sign contracts with each other enjoining parents to provide a ride home to their child (without the "third degree") when called and students not to accept a ride with someone drinking alcohol or using other drugs. One school had a Ralph Week honoring its custodian and encouraged students to keep their school neat and clean.

Cavender says that youth who will do well in the program generally have leadership skills and are highly motivated and creative. Characteristics of an effective adult sponsor include a healthy personality, high motivation, not overly controlling, and liked by students. Sponsors in this program include a high percentage of parents. Scheduling meetings—before or after school?—was a problem, according to Cavender, but he adds that STOP was the most effective program that they did.

SWAPP (Students Working Against Peer Pressure)

Bay City High School's SWAPP program began with thirty-five members and four sponsors, with major goals of making the school aware of SWAPP's existence and to decrease the alcohol problem. Initial training was funded by Bay City Chapter of Texans' War on Drugs.

Members regret that they got started late in the school year, which slowed them down, but they plan on having a dance and campaign to kick off the school year next fall. In fact, because of this late start, counselor Sallie Salas reports that the group has done extremely well with one-on-one and small-group interaction and support. She notes, "At meetings they seem to enjoy telling what they have done *themselves* to say no and how they have influenced others to say so." Even positive peer group members occasionally need additional support and reinforcement! Salas adds, "Most of the SWAPP students felt very proud to have been chosen to take part. It is the first time for many to be a part of a group at school."

Salas suggests that the optimal qualities of a youth for such a program are outgoingness (but not being pushy), willingness to listen, and awareness of those who need help. She says adult sponsors need to be someone who the youth have confidence in and respect for.

In one SWAPP activity members put up posters around the school with reminders of the negative effects of alcohol. One student, Michelle, says, "We had many slogans,...including 'Coors, Bud, and Miller can prove to be a killer' and 'Get high on life, not drugs.'" Another student, Heather, adds that "the SWAPP members signed a contract to avoid alcohol and other drugs." Also, a drawing was held at lunch time and door prizes were awarded in the name of SWAPP. The drawing was fun and created not only a lot of interaction but an awareness of their group. Another project involved helping youth "in crisis," whereby SWAPP members met individually with students who needed attention and encouragement.

TAD (Teens Against Drugs)

Every year McAllen area adult sponsors of
Teens Against Drugs hold a Super Saturday for
youth of junior high school age. I worked with
them on the May 1986 extravaganza, which drew
more than six hundred youth, ninety-five percent
of whom were Hispanic. Their goal was an awareness of dangers of drugs and their motto was
"Users Are Losers," which was attractively printed
on T-shirts that all the children received that day.
The event actually began on Friday, when I provided an all-day inservice seminar to more than fifty school staff members who learned more about
peer pressure reversal and the game plan for
Saturday.

Saturday's program was an all-day event (9:00
a.m. to 4:45 p.m.). The morning began with the
Presentation of Colors by the ROTC and wel-
comes by the mayor and school district superintendent. A short antidrug film was shown. I then
presented a fast-paced keynote address to all
youth on skills of resisting negative peer pressure.
At the end of my talk I asked for two football
players to volunteer to come on stage with me to
demonstrate the skills I had discussed. I motioned
to the two Dallas Cowboy football players back-
stage whom the youth knew would be there but
had not yet seen. Of course, the kids went wild,
cheering! The Cowboys practiced with me how to
say no to alcohol and other drugs.

After a short refreshment break (donated by
local restaurants), the youth were assigned into
groups of twenty-five to a classroom to do role-

play skits under the leadership of one of the faculty whom I had trained the previous day. The Cowboys and I went to each room during the next hour to reinforce participation and encourage their practices on handling all kinds of negative peer pressure. They later regrouped for my feedback presentation (all positive, as they had done so well!), and then we had lunch together in the cafeteria.

That afternoon an emphasis was placed on health, fitness, and living a fun, chemical-free life. The Cowboys spoke to the youth. Then clinics were held with volunteer instructors in the areas of aerobics, basketball, volleyball, karate, modeling, body building, and cheerleading. Awards were given to the top three participants in each clinic.

The day closed with the final event: a basketball game between the McAllen junior high school teachers, the superintendent, and McAllen police officers against local television, radio, and newspaper personnel. Cheerleaders cheered throughout the game and local radio personalities served as announcers.

To assure a good attendance, the sponsors provided bus service between all the junior high schools and the rally. Besides the enthusiastic faculty, many community leaders, clubs, organizations, and businesses supported this worthwhile event. It was fun learning!

TRY (Teen Relations and You)

I have been working with students, faculty, and parents on the TRY program at Lake Travis Middle School near Austin for the past two years. The group's goal, as reflected by the name they chose, is to learn to interact positively with one another. Group members hope their efforts will reduce some of the problems they see at school, such as fighting on buses, gossip, and pressure to drink alcohol. Sponsor Kim Dohrer reports that this peer group is growing and going in the right direction. She adds that the community is becoming more aware of it now and that recognition has helped to motivate the group.

Students have performed peer pressure reversal skits for classmates and upper elementary school students at the nearby elementary school. They have also sponsored a Get Acquainted and Make a New Friend Day during lunch in the school's cafeteria. TRY members have also formed welcome teams to greet new students and introduce them to various school activities.

H₂O (Help to Others)

I spent three full days in August, before school started, working with one hundred fifty students and fifty adults on Ball High School's H_2O program. This was to be an extension of the Galveston Intervention and Support Teams (GIST) program that began in 1984.

The enrollment at Ball High School is 2,797: forty percent black, thirty-six percent Caucasian, twenty-three percent Hispanic, and one percent Asian and native American. We trained better than five percent of the student body. During the last eighteen months prior to this training, seven Ball High School students or recent dropouts had died. The causes included suicide, traffic accidents, drowning, and complications from epilepsy.

The first day of the workshop focused on training the sponsors. Present, of course, were faculty sponsors from Ball High School, but also two representatives from every Galveston area school campus and representatives from community organizations (Junior League, PTA, etc.). The purpose of having others present was to develop a trained core team in each school that might elect at a later date to develop a positive peer group.

The second day focused on my training the youth in small-group sessions in peer pressure reversal and rotating them among the sponsors who had been involved in the previous day's training. Some youth gained valuable insights about their ability to make decisions and about peer pressure. I vividly recall a sophomore girl wondering aloud in her group why her best girlfriend was encouraging her to have sex with her casual boy-friend in order to keep him. She could not under-stand why her girlfriend seemed almost desperate in pushing her to do this and said she felt it was not right. The group finally offered an idea: perhaps it was because her friend had already had sex with her own boyfriend and wanted to make it seem okay by having others do the same thing. The student felt relief that her decision was right and understood more about peer pressure.

The third day involved establishing action plans. Through small-group interaction the participants first defined the problems, then prioritized them, selected goals, and brainstormed for possible solutions that H_2O could sponsor. The group es-tablished five problem areas to work on: alcohol and other drugs, truancy, gossip and cliques, teen pregnancy, and dress code. The last half of this day the students selected which of these five areas they had the most interest in and worked on that particular topic.

Each of these six groups has had similar as well as different goals, ideas, expectations, and re-sults. Some programs were developed following crises in the community and others were devel-oped as preventive techniques. All have had var-ious degrees of success: those most successful were due consistently to strong adult leadership that can organize, motivate, and encourage. And, of course, a lot of hard work by adults and youth.

7.

AFTERWORD

Afterword

You now know the steps to develop a positive peer group in your school. Don't delay—get started now! You may get tired from the hard work, but the youth's energy will carry you. And the results will be well worth the effort.

Michelle, a student in the Bay City SWAPP group, sums it up: "All the above may take time, but if it wasn't worth it, we wouldn't be doing it. Many times I become aggravated at how slow it seems to be going, but then I look back. . .and realize we are doing pretty good. This program is one that is needed in all schools because making better schools makes better people, thus making the whole world a better place to live."

8.

APPENDIXES

8.

APPENDIXES

Appendix 1
Letter to Parent

Dear Parent:

Your son/daughter _____ has been selected to participate in the positive peer group program at _____ . The goal of this program is to equip students with additional skills to enable them to serve as role models for their classmates and be actively involved in various programs to:

1. Encourage positive interaction among students;
2. Support and identify the lonely or isolated students;
3. Help make other students aware of the dangers of alcohol and other drug use;
4. Other:
5. Other:

In order for this program to be effective, your son/daughter will be asked to participate in the training sessions to be held on _____ , attend the regularly scheduled meetings, follow school rules, and not to use alcohol or other drugs.

Please acknowledge by the form below and have your child return it no later than _____ . If you have any questions about the program, please call me at _____ . Thank you.

Sincerely,

☐ I agree for my child to participate in the positive peer group.

☐ I do not agree for my child to participate in the positive peer group.

Signed _____

Date _____

Appendix 2

Positive Peer Group Application

I, _____ , wish to participate in
the positive peer group at my school. I realize that
for this group to be successful in its efforts to help
the student body, I must strive to be a good role
model. This includes:

1. Following school rules;

2. Complete the positive peer group training;

3. Attend the regularly scheduled meetings of
   this group;

4. Be involved in goal setting and development
   of programs that this group decides upon;

5. Not use alcohol or other drugs.

Signed _____

Date _____

Appendix 3

Action Plan

1. List at least five problems that exist in this school that the positive peer group needs to work on.

2. Are there any obvious obstacles to working on any of these problems?

3. Through group discussion, narrow the goals down to which ones the group wants to begin working on.

4. List as many ways as possible to approach the problems.

5. List any resources (people, material, etc.) that can be used as aids in solving the problems.

6. Specifically, write down how the group is going to approach each problem. Add who is to do what and by what day.

Appendix 4

Publicity

Get publicity for your group by contacting your local newspaper and radio and television stations. Also, publish an article in your school district newspaper.

Inform the student body of the development of the positive peer group and its goals. Invite students to attend some of the training. Prepare a typed press release for them and include comments by some of the students. Then recontact them thirty to ninety days later to do a follow-up piece recounting exactly what the students have done to accomplish their goals.

Enter contests whereby your group could receive recognition for its efforts (e.g., *Reader's Digest* contest for best posters on drug/alcohol dangers).

Appendix 5

HUMAN SUPPORT AWARD

_____ has earned this award for _____

Signed _____

Date _____

Positive Peer Group Training has been

successfully completed by

CONGRATULATIONS

School   Date   Sponsor

Appendix 7

Resources

Following are resources to obtain further information. Many sponsor youth conferences and publish newsletters containing good ideas.

America's PRIDE and College Challenge
c/o National Parents' Resource Institute for Drug Education
100 Edgewood Avenue, Suite 1002
Atlanta, GA 30303

National Federation of Parents for Drug-Free Youth
8730 Georgia Avenue, Suite 200
Silver Spring, MD 20910

Winners and Listen Magazines
c/o Narcotics Education, Inc.
6830 Laurel Street NW
Washington, DC 20012

The Just Say No Foundation
1777 North California Boulevard, Suite 200
Walnut Creek, CA 94596

Committees of Correspondence, Inc.
57 Conant Street, Room 113
Danvers, MA 09123

National Institute on Drug Abuse
5600 Fishers Lane, Room 10-A-43
Rockville, MD 20852

National Institute on Alcoholism and Alcohol Abuse
P.O. Box 2345
Rockville, MD 20852

Families in Action National Drug Information Center
3845 North Druid Hills Road, Suite 300
Decatur, GA 30033

Texans' War on Drugs
11044 Research Boulevard, Building D
Austin, TX 78759-5239
(for peer groups in Texas)

PRIDE Canada
College of Pharmacy, Suite 11
University of Saskatchewan
Saskatoon, Saskatchewan 57NOWO

Appendix 8

Sharon Scott and her associates are available in the following capacities:

- Keynote speaking
- Training youth and sponsors of positive peer groups
- Consultant on developing one- to five-year plans to combat drug use
- Workshop leader on various topics for adults and youth
- Purchase of video *Like a Roaring Lion*, which features Scott and an overview of her techniques (video is a dramatic film for teens on managing difficult peer pressure situations, including drugs, alcohol, and sex)
- "Positive Parenting" columns for school districts' newsletters

Write for further information:
Sharon Scott and Associates
5521 Hidalgo Court
Garland, Texas 75043

For information on ordering Scott's books:

- *Peer Pressure Reversal: An Adult Guide to Developing a Responsible Child*
- *How to Say No and Keep Your Friends*
- *Positive Peer Groups*
- *When to Say Yes!* (available spring 1988)

contact:
Human Resource Development Press
22 Amherst Road
Amherst, MA 01002
1-800-822-2801 (outside MA)
(413) 253-3488 (within MA)

Discounts given on quantity orders.

NOTES

NOTES